Name: _____

VOCABULARY
notebook

D1736600

Intentional Vocabulary Practice

Space to Practice 100 Words

Flexible for Early or Advanced Learners

ART + BOOKS + NATURE

FIRST EDITION

www.theschoolnest.com

Ideas for Vocabulary Exploration:

1. Discuss the word aloud together, using everyday language.
2. Write the definition.
3. Write the meaning in your own words.
4. Illustrate the meaning of the word, or an example of the word. Make it silly if it helps! It doesn't have to be artistic - stick figures work.
5. Use it in a sentence you create.
6. Copy a passage from a book that uses the vocabulary word.
7. Explore the parts of the word (prefix, root, suffix).
8. Use a thesaurus to find synonyms (same meaning) and antonyms (opposite meaning) and think of an example and non-example of the word.
9. Explain it to someone else, act out the word, use it in your daily conversation.
10. Flip back through your notebook every once in a while to review old words multiple times. Use the review check boxes to track your review sessions.

Using Your Notebook:

This isn't a workbook that needs every section completed. Each step is a tool to use at your current level of vocabulary work. With younger students, scribe for them as they put the definition into their own words and have them focus on drawing the meaning, acting it out, and reviewing. Older students can extend their work with the word onto the second page using more advanced skills.

Vocabulary Resources:

Use these resources to help you with some sections of the notebook.
- vocabulary.com: find lists of vocabulary words from any book, along with definitions, sentences from the book and other books, and synonyms.
- thesaurus.com: find your synonyms and antonyms
- litinfocus.com / 120-root-words-prefixes-and-suffixes-pdf-list: a nice alphabetized list of 120 word parts, meanings, and example words

1

2

3

4

5

6

7

8

9

10

11

12

13

14

15

Vocabulary Word List

16

17

18

19

20

21

22

23

24

25

26

27

28

28

30

31

32

33

34

35

36

37

38

39

40

41

42

43

44

45

Vocabulary Word List

46

47

48

49

50

51

52

53

54

55

56

57

58

59

60

Vocabulary Word List

61

62

63

64

65

66

67

68

69

70

71

72

73

74

75

Vocabulary Word List

76

77

78

79

80

81

82

83

84

85

86

87

88

89

90

91

92

93

94

95

96

97

98

99

100

eyrie

Eagle's eyrie - The Hobbit Pg 100

definition: The nest of an Eagle or other bird Prey built in a high inaccessible Place

in my own words: Eagle's nest

draw the word:

review: ☐ ☐ ☐ ☐ ☐

use in a sentence:

copywork:

| prefix | root | suffix |

synonyms	antonyms

example	non-example

definition:

in my own words:

draw the word:

use in a sentence:

copywork:

word study:

| prefix | root | suffix |

synonyms	antonyms
example	non-example

definition:

in my own words:

draw the word:

use in a sentence:

copywork:

prefix	root	suffix

synonyms	antonyms

example	non-example

definition:

in my own words:

draw the word:

review:

use in a sentence:

copywork:

| prefix | root | suffix |

synonyms	antonyms

example	non-example

definition:

in my own words:

draw the word:

☐ ☐ ☐ ☐ ☐

use in a sentence:

copywork:

prefix	root	suffix

synonyms	antonyms

example	non-example

definition:

in my own words:

draw the word:

☐ ☐ ☐ ☐ ☐

use in a sentence:

copywork:

| prefix | root | suffix |

synonyms	antonyms

example	non-example

definition:

in my own words:

draw the word:

use in a sentence:

copywork:

| prefix | root | suffix |

synonyms	antonyms

example	non-example

definition:

in my own words:

draw the word:

use in a sentence:

copywork:

prefix	root	suffix

synonyms	antonyms

example	non-example

definition:

in my own words:

draw the word:

use in a sentence:

copywork:

| prefix | root | suffix |

synonyms	antonyms
example	non-example

definition:

in my own words:

draw the word:

☐ ☐ ☐ ☐ ☐

use in a sentence:

copywork:

| prefix | root | suffix |

synonyms	antonyms
example	**non-example**

definition:

in my own words:

draw the word:

☐ ☐ ☐ ☐ ☐

use in a sentence:

copywork:

prefix	root	suffix

synonyms	antonyms

example	non-example

definition:

in my own words:

draw the word:

use in a sentence:

copywork:

prefix	root	suffix

synonyms	antonyms
example	non-example

definition:

in my own words:

draw the word:

☐ ☐ ☐ ☐ ☐

use in a sentence:

copywork:

| prefix | root | suffix |

synonyms	antonyms

example	non-example

definition:

in my own words:

draw the word:

use in a sentence:

copywork:

word study:

prefix	root	suffix

synonyms	antonyms

example	non-example

definition:

in my own words:

draw the word:

use in a sentence:

copywork:

prefix	root	suffix

synonyms	antonyms

example	non-example

definition:

in my own words:

draw the word:

use in a sentence:

copywork:

| prefix | root | suffix |

synonyms	antonyms

example	non-example

definition:

in my own words:

draw the word:

use in a sentence:

copywork:

prefix	root	suffix

synonyms	antonyms

example	non-example

definition:

in my own words:

draw the word:

☐ ☐ ☐ ☐ ☐

use in a sentence:

copywork:

| prefix | root | suffix |

synonyms	antonyms

example	non-example

definition:

in my own words:

draw the word:

☐ ☐ ☐ ☐ ☐

use in a sentence:

copywork:

| prefix | root | suffix |

synonyms	antonyms

example	non-example

definition:

in my own words:

draw the word:

use in a sentence:

copywork:

| prefix | root | suffix |

synonyms	antonyms

example	non-example

definition:

in my own words:

draw the word:

use in a sentence:

copywork:

| prefix | root | suffix |

synonyms	antonyms

example	non-example

definition:

in my own words:

draw the word:

use in a sentence:

copywork:

| prefix | root | suffix |

synonyms	antonyms

example	non-example

definition:

in my own words:

draw the word:

use in a sentence:

copywork:

word study:

| prefix | root | suffix |

synonyms	antonyms

example	non-example

definition:

in my own words:

draw the word:

use in a sentence:

copywork:

| prefix | root | suffix |

synonyms	antonyms

example	non-example

definition:

in my own words:

draw the word:

use in a sentence:

copywork:

word study:

prefix	root	suffix

synonyms	antonyms

example	non-example

definition:

in my own words:

draw the word:

use in a sentence:

copywork:

prefix	root	suffix

synonyms	antonyms

example	non-example

definition:

in my own words:

draw the word:

use in a sentence:

copywork:

| prefix | root | suffix |

synonyms	antonyms

example	non-example

definition:

in my own words:

draw the word:

use in a sentence:

copywork:

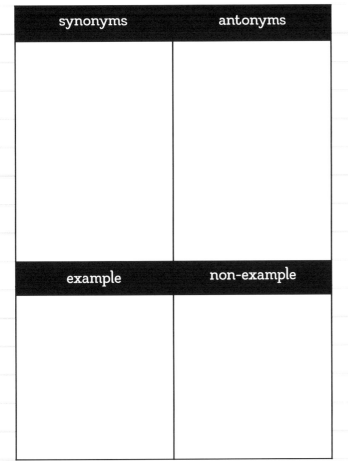

prefix   root   suffix

synonyms	antonyms

example	non-example

definition:

in my own words:

draw the word:

use in a sentence:

copywork:

prefix	root	suffix

synonyms	antonyms

example	non-example

definition:

in my own words:

draw the word:

use in a sentence:

copywork:

| prefix | root | suffix |

synonyms	antonyms

example	non-example

definition:

in my own words:

draw the word:

use in a sentence:

copywork:

| prefix | root | suffix |

synonyms	antonyms

example	non-example

definition:

in my own words:

draw the word:

☐ ☐ ☐ ☐ ☐

use in a sentence:

copywork:

| prefix | root | suffix |

synonyms	antonyms

example	non-example

definition:

in my own words:

draw the word:

use in a sentence:

copywork:

| prefix | root | suffix |

synonyms	antonyms

example	non-example

definition:

in my own words:

draw the word:

use in a sentence:

copywork:

| prefix | root | suffix |

synonyms	antonyms

example	non-example

definition:

in my own words:

draw the word:

☐ ☐ ☐ ☐ ☐

use in a sentence:

copywork:

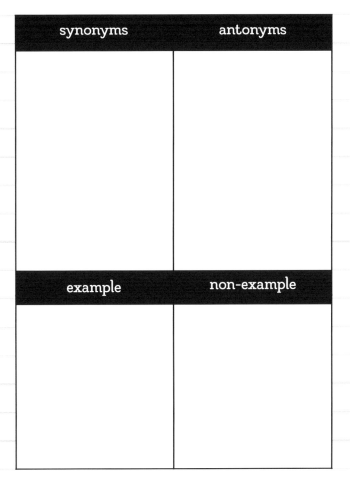

| prefix | root | suffix |

synonyms	antonyms

example	non-example

word 36

definition:

in my own words:

draw the word:

review: ☐ ☐ ☐ ☐ ☐

use in a sentence:

copywork:

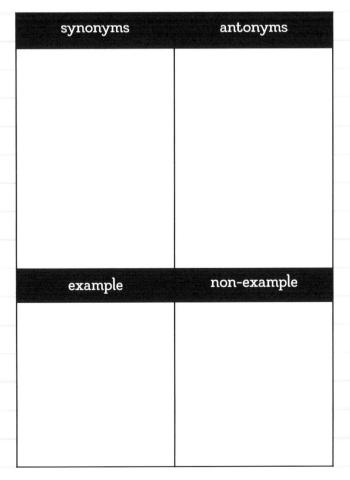

| prefix | root | suffix |

synonyms	antonyms

example	non-example

definition:

in my own words:

draw the word:

use in a sentence:

copywork:

| prefix | root | suffix |

synonyms	antonyms

example	non-example

definition:

in my own words:

draw the word:

use in a sentence:

copywork:

| prefix | root | suffix |

synonyms	antonyms

example	non-example

definition:

in my own words:

draw the word:

use in a sentence:

copywork:

prefix	root	suffix

synonyms	antonyms

example	non-example

definition:

in my own words:

draw the word:

review:

use in a sentence:

copywork:

| prefix | root | suffix |

synonyms	antonyms

example	non-example

definition:

in my own words:

draw the word:

use in a sentence:

copywork:

| prefix | root | suffix |

synonyms	antonyms

example	non-example

definition:

in my own words:

draw the word:

use in a sentence:

copywork:

| prefix | root | suffix |

synonyms	antonyms

example	non-example

definition:

in my own words:

draw the word:

review: ☐ ☐ ☐ ☐ ☐

use in a sentence:

copywork:

| prefix | root | suffix |

synonyms	antonyms

example	non-example

definition:

in my own words:

draw the word:

review:

use in a sentence:

copywork:

word study:

| prefix | root | suffix |

synonyms	antonyms

example	non-example

definition:

in my own words:

draw the word:

☐ ☐ ☐ ☐ ☐

use in a sentence:

copywork:

| prefix | root | suffix |

synonyms	antonyms

example	non-example

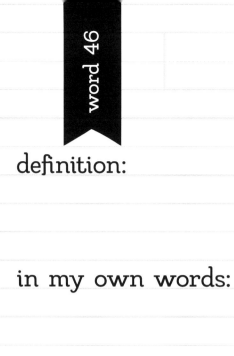

definition:

in my own words:

draw the word:

use in a sentence:

copywork:

| prefix | root | suffix |

synonyms	antonyms

example	non-example

definition:

in my own words:

draw the word:

☐ ☐ ☐ ☐ ☐

use in a sentence:

copywork:

| prefix | root | suffix |

synonyms	antonyms

example	non-example

definition:

in my own words:

draw the word:

use in a sentence:

copywork:

word study:

| prefix | root | suffix |

synonyms	antonyms

example	non-example

definition:

in my own words:

draw the word:

use in a sentence:

copywork:

| prefix | root | suffix |

synonyms	antonyms

example	non-example

definition:

in my own words:

draw the word:

use in a sentence:

copywork:

| prefix | root | suffix |

synonyms	antonyms

example	non-example

definition:

in my own words:

draw the word:

use in a sentence:

copywork:

| prefix | root | suffix |

synonyms	antonyms

example	non-example

definition:

in my own words:

draw the word:

review:

☐ ☐ ☐ ☐ ☐

use in a sentence:

copywork:

prefix	root	suffix

synonyms	antonyms

example	non-example

definition:

in my own words:

draw the word:

review:

use in a sentence:

copywork:

| prefix | root | suffix |

synonyms	antonyms

example	non-example

definition:

in my own words:

draw the word:

use in a sentence:

copywork:

| prefix | root | suffix |

synonyms	antonyms

example	non-example

definition:

in my own words:

draw the word:

use in a sentence:

copywork:

| prefix | root | suffix |

synonyms	antonyms

example	non-example

definition:

in my own words:

draw the word:

use in a sentence:

copywork:

| prefix | root | suffix |

synonyms	antonyms

example	non-example

definition:

in my own words:

draw the word:

use in a sentence:

copywork:

| prefix | root | suffix |

synonyms	antonyms

example	non-example

definition:

in my own words:

draw the word:

use in a sentence:

copywork:

| prefix | root | suffix |

synonyms	antonyms

example	non-example

definition:

in my own words:

draw the word:

use in a sentence:

copywork:

prefix	root	suffix

synonyms	antonyms

example	non-example

definition:

in my own words:

draw the word:

use in a sentence:

copywork:

word study:

| prefix | root | suffix |

synonyms	antonyms

example	non-example

definition:

in my own words:

draw the word:

use in a sentence:

copywork:

prefix	root	suffix

synonyms	antonyms

example	non-example

definition:

in my own words:

draw the word:

use in a sentence:

copywork:

| prefix | root | suffix |

synonyms	antonyms

example	non-example

definition:

in my own words:

draw the word:

use in a sentence:

copywork:

| prefix | root | suffix |

synonyms	antonyms

example	non-example

definition:

in my own words:

draw the word:

use in a sentence:

copywork:

| prefix | root | suffix |

synonyms	antonyms

example	non-example

definition:

in my own words:

draw the word:

use in a sentence:

copywork:

word study:

| prefix | root | suffix |

synonyms	antonyms

example	non-example

definition:

in my own words:

draw the word:

use in a sentence:

copywork:

| prefix | root | suffix |

synonyms	antonyms

example	non-example

definition:

in my own words:

draw the word:

use in a sentence:

copywork:

word study:

prefix	root	suffix

synonyms	antonyms

example	non-example

definition:

in my own words:

draw the word:

use in a sentence:

copywork:

prefix	root	suffix

synonyms	antonyms

example	non-example

definition:

in my own words:

draw the word:

review:

use in a sentence:

copywork:

word study:

prefix	root	suffix

synonyms	antonyms

example	non-example

definition:

in my own words:

draw the word:

use in a sentence:

copywork:

prefix	root	suffix

synonyms	antonyms

example	non-example

definition:

in my own words:

draw the word:

use in a sentence:

copywork:

prefix	root	suffix

synonyms	antonyms

example	non-example

definition:

in my own words:

draw the word:

review:

☐ ☐ ☐ ☐ ☐

use in a sentence:

copywork:

word study:

prefix	root	suffix

synonyms	antonyms

example	non-example

definition:

in my own words:

draw the word:

☐ ☐ ☐ ☐ ☐

use in a sentence:

copywork:

| prefix | root | suffix |

synonyms	antonyms

example	non-example

definition:

in my own words:

draw the word:

use in a sentence:

copywork:

| prefix | root | suffix |

synonyms	antonyms

example	non-example

definition:

in my own words:

draw the word:

use in a sentence:

copywork:

prefix	root	suffix

synonyms	antonyms

example	non-example

definition:

in my own words:

draw the word:

use in a sentence:

copywork:

| prefix | root | suffix |

synonyms	antonyms

example	non-example

definition:

in my own words:

draw the word:

review:

use in a sentence:

copywork:

| prefix | root | suffix |

synonyms	antonyms

example	non-example

definition:

in my own words:

draw the word:

use in a sentence:

copywork:

prefix	root	suffix

synonyms	antonyms

example	non-example

definition:

in my own words:

draw the word:

use in a sentence:

copywork:

| prefix | root | suffix |

synonyms	antonyms

example	non-example

definition:

in my own words:

draw the word:

use in a sentence:

copywork:

| prefix | root | suffix |

synonyms	antonyms

example	non-example

definition:

in my own words:

draw the word:

use in a sentence:

copywork:

| prefix | root | suffix |

synonyms	antonyms

example	non-example

definition:

in my own words:

draw the word:

☐ ☐ ☐ ☐ ☐

use in a sentence:

copywork:

| prefix | root | suffix |

synonyms	antonyms

example	non-example

definition:

in my own words:

draw the word:

use in a sentence:

copywork:

word study:

| prefix | root | suffix |

synonyms	antonyms

example	non-example

definition:

in my own words:

draw the word:

review:

use in a sentence:

copywork:

prefix	root	suffix

synonyms	antonyms

example	non-example

definition:

in my own words:

draw the word:

use in a sentence:

copywork:

prefix	root	suffix

synonyms	antonyms

example	non-example

definition:

in my own words:

draw the word:

use in a sentence:

copywork:

word study:

| prefix | root | suffix |

synonyms	antonyms

example	non-example

definition:

in my own words:

draw the word:

review:

use in a sentence:

copywork:

| prefix | root | suffix |

synonyms	antonyms

example	non-example

definition:

in my own words:

draw the word:

use in a sentence:

copywork:

word study:

prefix	root	suffix

synonyms	antonyms

example	non-example

definition:

in my own words:

draw the word:

review: ☐ ☐ ☐ ☐ ☐

use in a sentence:

copywork:

word study:

| prefix | root | suffix |

synonyms	antonyms

example	non-example

definition:

in my own words:

draw the word:

☐ ☐ ☐ ☐ ☐

use in a sentence:

copywork:

word study:

| prefix | root | suffix |

synonyms	antonyms

example	non-example

definition:

in my own words:

draw the word:

use in a sentence:

copywork:

prefix	root	suffix

synonyms	antonyms
example	non-example

definition:

in my own words:

draw the word:

use in a sentence:

copywork:

prefix	root	suffix

synonyms	antonyms

example	non-example

definition:

in my own words:

draw the word:

review:

use in a sentence:

copywork:

| prefix | root | suffix |

synonyms	antonyms

example	non-example

definition:

in my own words:

draw the word:

use in a sentence:

copywork:

prefix	root	suffix

synonyms	antonyms

example	non-example

definition:

in my own words:

draw the word:

use in a sentence:

copywork:

word study:

| prefix | root | suffix |

synonyms	antonyms

example	non-example

definition:

in my own words:

draw the word:

use in a sentence:

copywork:

word study:

prefix	root	suffix

synonyms	antonyms

example	non-example

definition:

in my own words:

draw the word:

☐ ☐ ☐ ☐ ☐

use in a sentence:

copywork:

prefix	root	suffix

synonyms	antonyms

example	non-example

definition:

in my own words:

draw the word:

☐ ☐ ☐ ☐ ☐

use in a sentence:

copywork:

| prefix | root | suffix |

synonyms	antonyms

example	non-example

definition:

in my own words:

draw the word:

review:

use in a sentence:

copywork:

| prefix | root | suffix |

synonyms	antonyms

example	non-example

definition:

in my own words:

draw the word:

☐ ☐ ☐ ☐ ☐

use in a sentence:

copywork:

| prefix | root | suffix |

synonyms	antonyms

example	non-example

Made in the USA
Las Vegas, NV
06 August 2021